Noah and the Mighty Ark

Rhonda Gowler Greene

Illustrated by Margaret Spengler

ZONDERKIDZ

Noah and the Mighty Ark
Copyright © 2007 by Rhonda Gowler Greene
Illustrations © 2014 by Margaret Spengler

This title is also available as a Zondervan ebook.
Visit www.zondervan.com/ebooks.

Requests for information should be addressed to:
Zonderkidz, 3900 *Sparks Dr, Grand Rapids, Michigan 49546*

ISBN 978-0-310-73217-4

Editor: Barbara Herndon
Art direction & design: Mary pat Pino

Printed in China

14 15 16 17 18 /LPC/ 10 9 8 7 6 5 4 3 2 1

God said to Noah ... "Make yourself an ark out
of cypress wood ... bring two of every living
thing into the ark."

Taken from Genesis 6:14–19

For my daughter, Lianna, who loves all animals, little or big.
—RGG

In memory of my loving mom, Jane.
—MS

God said,
"I will find
one good man,
strong and kind."

He found Noah,
said to him,
"Build an ark
and rooms within."

Then God said,
"When you're through,
bring the creatures
two by two."

So Noah did. He built a boat
lined with pitch so it would float.

It stood tall beneath the sun,
but Noah knew he wasn't done.

His sons brought water,
seed, and hay.
They filled the ark
by night and day.

Then,
he called the creatures two by two—
the elephant and kangaroo,

the crocodile,
the chimpanzee,
the busy *buzzing* bumblebee,

the tiny gnat,
the BIG, BLACK BEAR.
From far and wide, he called each pair

that crept or crawled
or hopped or flew
or stomped or tromped, or s-s-slithered too.

Yes, every creature
crowded in
and filled that ark
up to the brim

while up above
that giant ark,
the sky was growing
very dark!

Then—lightning *flash!*
And thunder **ROAR!**
When all were in,
God shut the door.

And so the rain
began—*plip-plop!*—
a rain that seemed to never stop.

For forty days
and nights the same—
plip-plop!—
the rain just came and came!

The water
s-W-E-L-L-E-D
to a great height
and covered everything in sight.

Those creatures, cramped
and squeezed inside,
huddled on that rocky ride.

Some *sh-sh-shivered.*
Some were filled with fear.
But Noah gently drew them near.

Then ...

whoosh! wind filled the sky,
made land turn dry,
and finally...

the sun appeared!

And Ararat, a mountain steep,
became a perch from waters deep.

Then,
a fine white dove sent on its way
returned with hope one sun-kissed day.

And creatures in that mighty ark
all lined up to disembark.

They crept. They crawled.
They hopped. They flew.
They left that huge ark two by two.

God said, "Now go
and multiply."

As Noah told each one goodbye,
God's rainbow promise . . .
filled the sky.